D1413239

THINGS TO
PRAY 5
FOR YOUR
HEART

RACHEL JONES

SERIES EDITOR: CARL LAFERTON

the good book
COMPANY

5 things to pray for your heart
Prayers that change you to be more like Jesus
© The Good Book Company, 2018. Reprinted 2018.
Series Editor: Carl Laferton

Published by
The Good Book Company
Tel (UK): 0333 123 0880
Tel (North America): (1) 866 244 2165
International: +44 (0) 208 942 0880
Email (UK): info@thegoodbook.co.uk
Email (North America): info@thegoodbook.com

Websites
UK & Europe: www.thegoodbook.co.uk
North America: www.thegoodbook.com
Australia: www.thegoodbook.com.au
New Zealand: www.thegoodbook.co.nz

ISBN: 9781784982829 | Printed in Denmark

Design by André Parker

CONTENTS

PRAYING FOR GROWTH WHEN I'M...

SERIES INTRODUCTION

I wonder if you have ever struggled to believe this famous verse from the Bible?

> *"The prayer of a righteous person is powerful and effective." (James 5 v 16)*

James is telling us that when righteous people pray righteous prayers, things happen. Things change. The prayers of God's people are powerful. But they are not powerful because we are powerful, or because the words we say are somehow magic, but because the Person we pray to is infinitely, unimaginably powerful. And our prayers are effective—not because we are special, or because there is a special formula to use, but because the God we pray to delights to answer our prayers and change the world because of them.

So what is the secret of effective prayer—how can you pray prayers that really change things? James suggests two questions that we need to ask ourselves.

First, are you righteous? A righteous person is someone who is in right relationship with God—someone who, through faith in Jesus, has been forgiven and accepted as a child of God. Are you someone who, as you pray, is praying not just to your Maker, not just to your Ruler, but to your heavenly Father, who has completely forgiven you through Jesus?

Second, do your prayers reflect that relationship? If we know God is our Maker, our Ruler and our Father, we will want to pray prayers that please him, that reflect his desires, that line up with his priorities for our lives and for the world. The kind of prayer that truly changes things is the prayer offered by a child of God that reflects God's heart.

That's why, when God's children pray in the Bible, we so often find them using the word of God to guide their prayers. So when Jonah prayed in the belly of a fish to thank God for rescuing him (Jonah 2 v 1-9), he used the words of several psalms strung together. When the first Christians gathered in Jerusalem to pray, they used the themes of Psalm 2 to guide their praise and their requests (Acts 4 v 24-30). And when Paul prayed that his friends would grow in love (Philippians 1 v 9), he was asking the Father to work in them the same thing the Lord Jesus prayed for us (John 17 v 25-26), and which the Holy Spirit is doing for all believers (Romans 5 v 5). They all used God's words to guide their words to God.

How can you pray prayers that are powerful and effective—that change things, that make things happen? First, by being a child of God. Second, by praying Bible prayers, which use God's words to make sure your prayers are pleasing to him and share his priorities.

That's what this little book is here to help you with. It will guide you on how to pray for yourself, in 21 different areas and situations. Praying for yourself may seem a little self-indulgent! But these are not self-centred prayers. As you pray that you would become more and more the person that God created and saved you to be—and as God answers those prayers—he will be more greatly glorified in you, and those around you will be more lovingly served by you. And, yes, you will experience the blessing that it is to live like Jesus.

Each prayer suggestion is based on a passage of the Bible, so you can be certain that they are prayers that God wants you to pray for yourself.

There are five different things to pray for each of the 21 areas. So you can use this book in a variety of ways.

- *You can pray a set of "five things" each day, over the course of three weeks, and then start again.*

- *You can take one of the prayer themes and pray a part of it every day from Monday to Friday.*

- *Or you can dip in and out of it, as and when you want and need to pray for a particular aspect of your life.*

- *There's also a space on each page for you to write in the names of specific situations, concerns or people that you intend to remember in prayer.*

This is by no means an exhaustive guide—there are plenty more things that you can be praying for your life as you seek to live God's way in God's world!

But you can be confident as you use it that you are praying great prayers—prayers that God wants you to pray. And God promises that "the prayer of a righteous person is powerful and effective". That's a promise that is worth grasping hold of confidently. As we pray trusting this promise, it will change how we pray and what we expect to come from our prayers.

When righteous people pray righteous prayers, things happen. Things change. So as you use this book to guide your prayers, be excited, be expectant, and keep your eyes open for God to do "immeasurably more than all we ask or imagine" (Ephesians 3 v 20). He's powerful; and so your prayers are too.

Carl Laferton
Editorial Director | The Good Book Company

LOVE

MARK 12 v 29-31

PRAYER POINTS:

_____

_____

_____

_____

Father in heaven, help me to love...

 ONE GOD

> *"The most important [commandment] ... is
> this: 'Hear, O Israel: the Lord our God, the
> Lord is one'" (v 29).*

God is the only one truly worthy of all our love and
affection. All other rivals pale in comparison with his
power and glory. But we don't worship him from a
distance—he is "the Lord *our* God", because he has
set his love upon us and included us among his people. We love him because he has loved us. So praise
him for his complete power and tender care.

 WITH MY HEART AND SOUL

> *"Love the Lord your God with all your heart
> and with all your soul" (v 30).*

Pray that you would love God with all of your affec-
tions—that you would relate to him in a way that really affects how you *feel* about him. Confess the ways
in which you love other things too much—ask God to
make himself your first love.

WITH MY MIND

"... with all your mind" (v 30).

When we love someone, we think about them. Pray that God would increasingly fill your mind; that he'd be your first thought in the morning, your last thought at night and your constant companion in the hours between. Thank God for giving you a brain with which to think—pray that everything you learn *about* God would fuel your love *for* God.

 WITH MY STRENGTH

"... with all your strength" (v 30).

When does your love for God tend to feel most feeble? In what area have you grown weary? When is your service of him half-hearted? Ask God to help you to love him with all of your strength—so that every day you would willingly and joyfully spend whatever energy you have for his glory.

 ... AND MY NEIGHBOUR

"'Love your neighbour as yourself.' There is no commandment greater than these" (v 31).

We don't truly love God if we don't love those around us. Pray that you would pursue the good of others as though their interests were yours. Think through those you will interact with today, and ask God to help you to love each one. And thank him for his love for you—that he loves you with this kind of all-consuming love.

JOY

PSALM 16

PRAYER POINTS:

_____

_____

_____

_____

Father, please give me great joy in...

 THE GIVER, NOT THE GIFTS

> *"You are my Lord; apart from you I have no*
> *good thing" (v 2).*

God is *your* Lord and Father through faith in Christ—
pray that this truth would be your greatest joy in life.
Confess the times when you've chased after happiness
in good things, instead of pursuing joy in a good God.

 BEING PART OF YOUR PEOPLE

> *"I say of the holy people who are in the*
> *land, 'They are the noble ones in whom is*
> *all my delight'" (v 3).*

Ask God to give you increasing joy in being one of his
"holy people". Thank God for your church family, and
for some specific Christians who particularly encourage you. Pray that your joy would be fuelled Sunday
by Sunday as you meet with God's people. Ask God
to open your eyes to see how other people are growing in godliness and using their gifts—pray that these
signs of God's grace would cause your heart to rejoice.

WHAT YOU HAVE GIVEN ME

> *"The boundary lines have fallen for me in pleasant places; surely I have a delightful inheritance" (v 6).*

Give thanks for the things God has given you that you take delight in—big or small. List as many as you can! Pray for greater contentment with what you have.

 ## HARD TIMES

> *"I keep my eyes always on the LORD. With him at my right hand, I shall not be shaken" (v 8).*

Ask God to grow in you a deep-seated, unshakeable joy that no difficulty or disappointment can snatch from you. Pray that when suffering comes, his presence beside you would continue to give you joy.

 ## ETERNAL LIFE

> *"Therefore my heart is glad and my tongue rejoices ... You make known to me the path of life; you will fill me with joy in your presence, with eternal pleasures at your right hand" (v 9, 11).*

Give thanks that Jesus' resurrection, which this psalm points forward to (Acts 2 v 24-28), guarantees your own—he's paved the way to eternal life. Rejoice that one day you will experience a joy deeper than you've ever known, in the presence of your Saviour. Pray that this promise would shape how you feel today.

PEACE

ISAIAH 41 v 8-14

PRAYER POINTS:

_____

_____

_____

_____

*These promises were given first to the people of Is-
rael, then fulfilled in Christ, and now are extended
to all his people today. So ask God to grow in you a
deep inner confidence in...*

 YOUR LOVE FOR ME

> *"I took you from the ends of the earth,
> from its farthest corners I called you. I
> said, 'You are my servant'; I have chosen
> you and have not rejected you" (v 9).*

Thank God that he has chosen to love you and called
you to be one of his people, and always works for
your good. Praise him that he has never and will never
reject you, because you are "in Christ".

 YOUR PRESENCE WITH ME

> *"So do not fear, for I am with you; do not
> be dismayed, for I am your God" (v 10).*

What is it that you fear? What are the circumstances
that cause you dismay? Thank God that you do not
face these things alone—he is with you. Pray that
this truth would encourage your heart and give you a
great sense of peace.

YOUR INTERVENTION FOR ME

> *"I will strengthen you and help you; I will uphold you with my righteous right hand" (v 10).*

Ask God to be at work in and through the specific circumstances that trouble you. However you're feeling, pray that you would become more reliant on him, regularly turning to him in prayer for help.

 YOUR VINDICATION OF ME

> *"All who rage against you will surely be ashamed and disgraced; those who oppose you will be as nothing and perish" (v 11).*

Many of our worries are about other people—what they'll say, do or think. Thank God that he sees and cares about how his people are treated; pray that this knowledge would shape how you respond to others, no matter how they treat you. Pray that you would interact with people with godly confidence.

 YOUR SUPERIORITY TO ME

> *"'Do not be afraid, you worm Jacob, little Israel, do not fear, for I myself will help you,' declares the LORD, your Redeemer, the Holy One of Israel" (v 14).*

Sometimes our worries can be helpful—they remind us that we are "little" and not in control. So thank God that he is far greater than you. Pray that the knowledge that he is "your Redeemer" would give you peace.

PATIENCE

JAMES 5 v 7-11

PRAYER POINTS:

 PATIENT FOR CHRIST'S COMING

*"Be patient, then, brothers and sisters, until
the Lord's coming ... be patient and stand
firm" (v 7-8).*

In many ways, the Christian life is one long waiting
game—we're waiting for Christ to return to put right
all wrongs, and to prove once and for all that we've
been following the right King. But sometimes, when
we look around us, we doubt that day will ever come.
So ask God to make you patient. Pray for perseverance to stand firm in your faith for as long as it takes
for Jesus to return.

 PATIENT WITH MY WORDS

*"Don't grumble against one another, broth-
ers and sisters, or you will be judged" (v 9).*

Few things test our patience more than other people—and often Christians in particular. So pray that
you would be patient when other believers hurt you,
let you down, or just get on your nerves. Pray you
would not grumble against them—not to their faces,
nor behind their backs, nor even in your heart.

3 PATIENT IN MY WITNESS

"As an example of patience in the face of suffering, take the prophets who spoke in the name of the Lord" (v 10).

Is there someone you've given up trying to "speak in the name of the Lord" to, because they've rejected you so many times in the past? Pray that you would be a patient witness who seeks to speak about the Lord again and again, even when it's costly.

4 PATIENT WITH GOD

"As you know, we count as blessed those who have persevered. You have heard of Job's perseverance and have seen what the Lord finally brought about" (v 11).

"Why is God letting this happen?" "When will he change my circumstances?" "Why won't he answer my prayers?" Ask God to help you to be patient with his plans, and specifically with their timing. Pray for increasing confidence that God's ways always lead to blessing, even when you can't see how that can be.

5 PATIENT LIKE GOD

"The Lord is full of compassion and mercy" (v 11).

Thank God for how patient he is with you. When you are weak, he shows you compassion. When you are sinful, he shows you mercy. Thank him for specific ways in which you have experienced his patience recently.

KINDNESS

EPHESIANS 4 v 32 – 5 v 2

 KIND AND COMPASSIONATE

"Be kind and compassionate to one another" (v 32).

Ask God to give you a kind heart—one that reaches out to others to meet their needs and serve them practically. Pray you would be kind not just to those you naturally warm to but to *everyone* in your church family. Ask God to put in your path people who are in special need of a kind word or deed at the moment—and for eyes to see how you can show them kindness.

 ... TO THOSE WHO HURT ME

"... forgiving each other, just as in Christ God forgave you" (v 32).

Thank God for forgiving all your sin through Christ. Confess the ways in which you've failed to be kind to others, and rejoice in God's full and free forgiveness of those failings. Pray that as God has forgiven you, so you would forgive others. Ask God to help you to be kind in your thoughts towards those who have hurt you in the past; and—if possible and wise—kind in your actions too.

... LIKE MY FATHER

> *"Follow God's example, therefore, as dearly loved children" (v 1).*

Thank God for how kind he has been to you. He saw your need for salvation and he met it, adopting you as his own dearly loved child. Pray that this knowledge would liberate you to be kind to others—not so as to impress God or make other people like you but because you want to act like your heavenly Father.

 ... ALL THE TIME

> *"Live a life of love" (v 2).*

Sometimes, we want to do kindness on our own terms: only when we've got the energy for it, or only when we'll get noticed for it, or only when we're down on the rota for it. But this command is all-encompassing. Ask God to transform your heart so that serving others and offering help become your instinctive responses. Pray for an opportunity to be spontaneously kind to someone today.

 ... EVEN WHEN IT COSTS

> *"Just as Christ loved us and gave himself up for us as a fragrant offering and sacrifice to God" (v 2).*

Is there something particularly costly that God is calling you to at the moment? Pray that, like the Lord Jesus, you'd be prepared to love others even when that requires great personal sacrifice.

GOODNESS

ROMANS 12 v 9-13

PRAYER POINTS:

_____

_____

_____

_____

*At the heart of "goodness" is the idea of integrity—
we're called to hold to the truth and live it out without
any hint of hypocrisy. So pray that you would grow in…*

 SINCERE GOODNESS

"Love must be sincere" (v 9).

Ask God to help you to love others sincerely; pray
that you wouldn't care for people because you know
that you *should*, but because you *actually do*! Pray
that you'd love people both to their faces—saying to
them only what is truthful—and behind their backs—
saying about them only what is loving.

 DEEP GOODNESS

*"Hate what is evil; cling to what is good"
(v 9).*

Pray that you'd be less concerned with *looking* good
and more concerned with *being* good, right down
to your very core. Ask God to give you a growing
disgust at the things he hates—confess times when
you've treated sin as a bit funny, or not very serious.
Pray that you would prize holiness more highly.

PASSIONATE GOODNESS

"Never be lacking in zeal, but keep your spiritual fervour, serving the Lord" (v 11).

We live "in view of God's mercy" to us in Christ (v 1)—take some time to thank and praise him for his mercy now. Pray that God's grace to you at the cross would make you more excited about serving him today—and that this passion for Jesus would overflow in goodness towards others.

 CONSISTENT GOODNESS

"Be joyful in hope, patient in affliction, faithful in prayer" (v 12).

What circumstances are currently putting your character to the test? Ask God to help you to respond with solid joy, genuine patience and faithful prayer. Thank him for the great hope that the gospel gives.

 PRACTICAL GOODNESS

"Share with the Lord's people who are in need. Practise hospitality" (v 13).

Ask God to help you to do good to others in a way that practically meets their needs. Prayerfully think about how that might look for you this week. Ask God to help you be bold enough to step out of your comfort zone, in order to welcome others in. It's often in our homes that our true selves are revealed—pray that as people get to know you better, they would see a godly man or woman of complete integrity.

FAITHFULNESS

HEBREWS 12 v 1-3

PRAYER POINTS:

_____

_____

_____

_____

FAITHFUL WITNESSES

"Therefore, since we are surrounded by such a great cloud of witnesses..." (v 1).

Whose faithfulness inspires you? It might be characters from the Bible, heroes from church history, or Christians you know today. Give thanks for these "witnesses"—thank God for some specific ways in which they proved themselves faithful to Jesus, and in which Jesus proved himself faithful to them. Pray that you would follow their examples of courage, loyalty and truthfulness.

FAITHFUL FIGHTER

"Let us throw off everything that hinders and the sin that so easily entangles" (v 1).

Ask God to help you to fight the specific distractions that pull your heart away from him, and the sins that you get caught up in. Pray that you would live in wholehearted, undivided faithfulness to him. And ask for help in living out the "let *us*" in this verse—ask God to deepen your Christian friendships so that you increasingly confront and confess sin together.

FAITHFUL RUNNER

> *"And let us run with perseverance the race marked out for us" (v 1).*

How's the course that God's set for *you* looking? What are the obstacles that make you want to give up? Who are the teammates you're called to stick by and help along? Ask God to help you to persevere in following Jesus and serving his people in the specific circumstances he has marked out for you.

FAITHFUL KING

> *"… fixing our eyes on Jesus, the pioneer and perfecter of faith" (v 2).*

Thank Jesus that "for the joy that was set before him he endured the cross, scorning its shame" (v 2), so that you could be brought into God's family. Worship your King, who has now "sat down at the right hand of the throne of God". Thank him that his faithfulness to his Father and to his people knows no limits. Pray that you would keep your eyes fixed on him today.

FAITHFUL UNDER FIRE

> *"Consider him who endured such opposition from sinners, so that you will not grow weary and lose heart" (v 3).*

Ask God to give you an opportunity today to be a faithful witness to "sinners"—those who reject Jesus as King—around you. Pray for courage to be loyal to King Jesus when it would be easier to protect your reputation or pursue your comfort.

GENTLENESS

JOHN 13 v 12-17

PRAYER POINTS:

_____

_____

_____

_____

In the list of the fruit of the Spirit in Galatians 5, the King James Bible translates "gentleness" as "meekness". Outer gentleness is the way inner humility shows itself.

 GENTLE LIKE JESUS

> *"Do you understand what I have done for you?" (v 12).*

Jesus was so gentle with his words. The disciples were often slow to understand—yet Jesus didn't lord it over them, but instead explained patiently. Pray that you, too, would be gentle with your words, and resist saying things that are pointed, patronising or proud.

 GRATEFUL FOR JESUS

> *"Now that I, your Lord and Teacher, have washed your feet..." (v 14).*

Thank Jesus for doing something more humble even than washing the disciples' feet—thank him for cleansing your heart of sin. Marvel for a moment at his humility: that though he is the wisest teacher and the most powerful Lord, yet he was willing to live and die as a human in order to make you clean.

A SERVANT LIKE JESUS

"... you also should wash one another's feet. I have set you an example that you should do as I have done for you" (v 14-15).

Ask God to help you to serve others as Jesus has served you; pray you'd be ready to love others in a way that is gentle, messy, practical and personal.

 A SERVANT OF JESUS

"Very truly I tell you, no servant is greater than his master, nor is a messenger greater than the one who sent him" (v 16).

Ask God to help you to remember that you are only a servant, and that Jesus is master. Repent of ways in which an inflated sense of your own importance has led you to treat others harshly. Pray that you would be willing to do anything your master demands of you.

 BLESSED BY JESUS

"Now that you know these things, you will be blessed if you do them" (v 17).

Our culture says that the good life is found in achieving a position of power, wealth and influence; Jesus says that true blessing is found in using what power, wealth and influence we have to serve others. Give thanks for the ways in which you've experienced the blessing Jesus promises in this verse. Pray that your gentleness would make you a blessing to others, even as it blesses you.

SELF-CONTROL

TITUS 2 v 11-14

GIVE THANKS FOR GRACE

"For the grace of God has appeared that offers salvation to all people" (v 11).

Thank God that our salvation is not dependent on how much self-control we can exercise. He doesn't offer salvation only to moral people who can keep his rules. He offers salvation to "all people"; he's offered it to you. Thank God for his boundless grace, which continues to flow to us no matter how many times we fail him. Pray that the way you live would point those around you not to religious rule-keeping but to God's extraordinary offer of grace in Christ Jesus.

STRENGTH TO SAY "NO"

"It teaches us to say 'No' to ungodliness and worldly passions" (v 12).

What do you find it hardest to say "No" to? Maybe it's in the area of greed or anger or lust or gossip. Confess the moments when you've said "Yes" to un-godliness in the past few days. Pray that the next time you're faced with temptation, God would give you the self-control to say "No" instead.

GODLY INSTINCTS

*"... and to live self-controlled, upright and
godly lives in this present age" (v 12).*

Often the ungodly things we say are out of our
mouths before we've even thought about them.
Pray that God would transform your heart so that it
grows in self-control. Pray that your instinctive reactions would be increasingly upright and godly.

HOPEFUL EXPECTATION

*"... while we wait for the blessed hope—the
appearing of the glory of our great God
and Saviour, Jesus Christ, who gave himself for us to redeem us from all wickedness and to purify for himself a people that
are his very own" (v 13).*

Rejoice that a day is coming when Jesus will appear
and you will enjoy living with him in sinless perfection, completely free of temptation, failure and guilt.
Ask God to help you to live now in the light of this
"blessed hope".

EAGER TO DO GOOD

"... eager to do what is good" (v 14).

Often we reduce self-control to a dutiful act of willpower—instead, ask God to make you genuinely
eager to do what is good. Ask him to help you to
do good today. Pray for wisdom in setting the right
priorities, and for self-control to avoid distractions.

5 THINGS TO PRAY

PRAYING THAT I WOULD BE A

WORSHIPPER

PSALM 96

PRAYER POINTS:

_____

_____

_____

_____

 SING!

> *"Sing to the LORD a new song ... Proclaim his salvation day after day. Declare his glory among the nations, his marvellous deeds among all peoples" (v 1-3).*

Give thanks to God for his salvation through Jesus Christ. Praise him for his "marvellous deeds"—both those recorded in the pages of the Bible and those that have played out in your own life. Pray that your times of sung worship at church on Sunday would be a heartfelt response to God's "marvellous deeds".

 THE ONLY GOD

> *"Great is the LORD and most worthy of praise; he is to be feared above all gods. For all the gods of the nations are idols..." (v 4-5).*

Human beings can't help but worship—yet often the possessions, relationships or roles we have (or want to have) become our idols. We prize them as more worthy of our time, attention, praise, love or fear than the Lord. What idols are you worshipping? Repent of them before God.

ALMIGHTY CREATOR

"The LORD made the heavens" (v 5).

Thank God for all the good things he has made that you can see out of your window (even if you have to look hard to see the beauty!). Pray that living in God's created world would lead you to greater worship of its Creator.

 HOLY LORD

"Worship the LORD in the splendour of his holiness; tremble before him, all the earth" (v 9).

God is completely other than us, blistering in his holiness and purity. Thank him for the miracle that, through Christ, you are able to approach him personally. Yet this shouldn't mean we approach him casually— ask God to give you deeper appreciation of his holiness and a greater reverence towards him.

 RIGHTEOUS JUDGE

"Let all creation rejoice before the LORD, for he comes, he comes to judge the earth. He will judge the world in righteousness and the people in his faithfulness" (v 13).

God is coming to put the world to right—rejoice in that truth now. Thank him that we no longer need to fear his judgment because Christ has faced it on our behalf. Pray that this truth would lead you to live a life of grateful worship as you wait for his coming.

PRAYING THAT I WOULD BE A

LEARNER

PROVERBS 2 v 1-11

PRAYER POINTS:

_____

_____

_____

_____

Father, help me to be a learner who…

SEEKS WISDOM

"Turning your ear to wisdom and applying your heart to understanding … look for it as for silver and search for it as for hidden treasure" (v 2, 4).

Thank God for his precious wisdom. Ask God to give you a heart that longs to know him more deeply—that you'd pour all your effort and energy into becoming wiser in the things of God. Pray that you would treasure God's truth rightly and not take it for granted.

PRAYS FOR WISDOM

"If you call out for insight and cry aloud for understanding…" (v 3).

Pray that you will learn prayerfully, not proudly. Confess the times you've approached God's word with a misplaced confidence in your ability to understand it, rather than a conscious reliance on God's Spirit. When will you be hearing or reading God's word this week? Cry aloud for God to give you understanding.

FEARS THE LORD

"... then you will understand the fear of the LORD and find the knowledge of God" (v 5).

Pray that what you *know* about God would change how you *feel* about God. Ask that every sermon you listen to, passage you study or verse you read would increase your awe of the LORD'S majesty. Pray that you would be moved to worship by all that you learn.

LOOKS ONLY TO GOD

"For the LORD gives wisdom; from his mouth come knowledge and understanding" (v 6).

Thank God that he generously gives wisdom. We have the words of his mouth right in front of us in the Bible! As you listen to others, pray that you would be able to discern the voices offering godly wisdom from the voices offering worldly wisdom.

MAKES WISE CHOICES

"Then you will understand what is right and just and fair—every good path. For wisdom will enter your heart, and knowledge will be pleasant to your soul" (v 9-10).

Pray that what you learn would shape how you live. Ask the Lord to show you "what is right and just and fair", and then help you to actually do it! Pray through specific areas where you need wisdom at the moment. Ask God to guide you to "every good path".

PRAYING THAT I WOULD BE A

TEACHER

ACTS 18 v 24-28

PRAYER POINTS:

_____

_____

_____

_____

Everybody should be teaching somebody about Jesus. It might be our kids, a Sunday School class, a Bible study or simply speaking God's word into the lives of friends. Ask God to help you to be...

KNOWLEDGEABLE

> *"[Apollos] was a learned man, with a thorough knowledge of the Scriptures" (v 24).*

You cannot teach what you do not know. Thank God for equipping us with the Scriptures—pray that you would be growing in your own knowledge and love of the Bible day by day and week by week.

PASSIONATE

> *"He spoke with great fervour ... He began to speak boldly in the synagogue" (v 25).*

Pray that you would be a passionate teacher of God's word. Pray for courage to faithfully teach the whole truth—even the hard truth. Ask God to give you an infectious excitement about following Jesus, so that people would hear your words and want to follow him more wholeheartedly too.

TEACHABLE

"When Priscilla and Aquila heard him, they invited him to their home and explained to him the way of God more adequately"
(v 26).

Apollos was knowledgeable and passionate—but he still had something important to learn, and he was willing to learn it. Pray that you too would be a teachable teacher. Give thanks for those mature believers who have drawn alongside you to "explain the way of God" to you in the past. Ask for humility to receive feedback, correction and encouragement.

 A GREAT HELP

"He was a great help to those who by grace had believed" *(v 27).*

Pray that your teaching would bear fruit in others' lives. Think of some specific believers you have the opportunity to teach. What "help" do they need in their faith? Ask that your words would be of great help to them.

 JESUS-FOCUSED

"... proving from the Scriptures that Jesus was the Messiah" *(v 28).*

Pray that all your teaching would help people to understand the Scriptures and see who Jesus is and what he has done. Ask God to use you to bring people to acknowledge Jesus as the Messiah—God's ruling, rescuing King.

PRAYING THAT I WOULD BE AN

AMBASSADOR

EPHESIANS 6 v 10-20

PRAYER POINTS:

_____

_____

_____

_____

 FEARLESS AMBASSADOR

"Pray also for me, that whenever I speak, words may be given me so that I will fear-lessly make known the mystery of the gospel, for which I am an ambassador in chains" (v 19-20).

Thank God that he has given you a privileged role: he's made you an ambassador, a representative of Christ's kingdom in this world. As Paul does in these verses, ask God to give you the words to share it with others.

Heavenly Father, make me a gospel ambassador who is fearless because…

 I KNOW THE REAL ENEMY

"For our struggle is not against flesh and blood, but against … spiritual forces" (v 12).

Evangelism is hard because it's a spiritual battle—knowing all the right answers or loving people well isn't enough to win them for Christ. Pray that this would drive you to an increasing prayerful dependence on God, because you know you need his power.

I'M PROTECTED

"Stand firm then ... with the breastplate of righteousness in place" (v 14).

You're completely secure before God because you wear a breastplate of Christ's righteousness, not your own—thank and praise him for that. Pray that this knowledge would help you to stand firm for Jesus because you're loved and accepted by God, even if you're mocked and rejected by others.

 I'M READY

"... with your feet fitted with the readiness that comes from the gospel of peace" (v 15).

Pray that you would be ready to share the gospel of peace. Pray that you wouldn't duck out, dodge the question or change the topic of conversation. Instead, ask for courage to take—and even make—every opportunity to speak about Jesus. Ask him to give you one today (perhaps with someone unlikely).

 I'M ARMED

"Take the helmet of salvation and the sword of the Spirit, which is the word of God" (v 17).

Thank God that he's given us a weapon through which the Spirit will work in the lives of others: his word. Think of some non-Christians you know—how might you engage them with the Bible? Ask God to help you step out as his ambassador and speak his words to others.

5 THINGS TO PRAY

PRAYING THAT I WOULD BE A

FRIEND

LUKE 17 v 1-6

PRAYER POINTS:

_____

_____

_____

_____

Father, help me to be a friend to others who is...

 CAREFUL

> *"Things that cause people to stumble are bound to come, but woe to anyone through whom they come" (v 1).*

Ask for forgiveness for any way you've led your friends into sin. In doesn't take much—an off-colour joke, a snide remark, a bad attitude. Ask for grace to watch yourself (v 3). Pray that your words and example would spur your Christian friends towards godliness, and point your non-Christian friends towards Jesus.

 HONEST

> *"If your brother or sister sins against you, rebuke them" (v 3).*

Ask God to bless you with real, honest friendships. Pray that you would be humble enough to listen to your friends when they rebuke you, and loving enough to challenge your Christian friends over their sin and help them to grow more Christ-like. Pray you would love them more than you love their approval.

FORGIVING

"… and if they repent, forgive them" (v 3).

Thank God that he always forgives you when you repent—even though you sin against him far more than "seven times in a day" (v 4). So pray that you would be a friend who forgives—who decides to love, to act and to pray as though a wrong had never been committed. Is there another Christian you're withholding forgiveness from? Ask for a spirit of true forgiveness.

CHRIST-DEPENDENT

"The apostles said to the Lord, 'Increase our faith!'" (v 5).

Not all friendships are easy, and no friendship is easy all the time. So cry out to the Lord to give you what you need to be a good friend. Thank God for pouring his love into your heart so that you can show it to others—ask him to make you dependent on him.

PRAYERFUL

"If you have faith as small as a mustard seed, you can say to this mulberry tree, 'Be uprooted and planted in the sea,' and it will obey you" (v 6).

Jesus is clear: prayer works! So ask him to help you to be consistent and persistent in prayer on your friends' behalf. Think of one or two friends, and pray now for their specific situations. Ask God to fill them with faith in his promises.

PRAYING THAT I WOULD BE A

WORKER

PROVERBS 10 v 4-16

PRAYER POINTS:

_____

_____

_____

_____

Whether you work at a desk, on a production line, in the home or elsewhere, ask for help to work with...

DILIGENCE

> *"Lazy hands make for poverty, but diligent hands bring wealth" (v 4).*

It's a principle we see throughout Scripture: hard work honours God, and God honours hard work. We weren't created for a life of leisure—we were created to be productive. So ask for grace to see any ways in which you are approaching work with a lazy, grudging or half-hearted attitude. Ask God to enable you to enjoy the satisfaction of work done well.

WISDOM

> *"He who gathers crops in summer is a prudent son, but he who sleeps during harvest is a disgraceful son" (v 5).*

Perhaps you struggle to know what to focus your effort on, how to get the job done, or where you'll find the time. Ask God to give you wisdom—bring before him your particular work concerns.

3 HUMILITY

"The wise in heart accepts commands, but a chattering fool comes to ruin" (v 8).

Pray for your relationship with your boss (or anyone with authority over you). Ask God to give you a spirit of willing submission that humbly "accepts commands", even when you don't like them. Confess times when you have been a "chattering fool". Pray that you would speak *to* and *about* your co-workers with grace and self-control.

4 INTEGRITY

"Whoever walks in integrity walks securely, but whoever takes crooked paths will be found out" (v 9).

In what ways are you tempted to take shortcuts or act dishonestly? Pray that you would walk in integrity. Sometimes we get frustrated when we see crooked people "getting away with it". Thank God that one day everyone will be brought to account.

5 ETERNAL PRIORITIES

"The wages of the righteous is life, but the earnings of the wicked are sin and death" (v 16).

Thank God that although you deserve "the wages of sin", you've received "the gift of God ... eternal life in Christ" (Romans 6 v 23). Pray that this would affect the way you work, and mean more to you than your work.

PRAYING FOR GROWTH WHEN I'M

DOUBTING

1 JOHN 5 v 9-15

PRAYER POINTS:

_____

_____

_____

_____

Heavenly Father, when I'm doubting, help me to...

TRUST YOUR TESTIMONY

"We accept human testimony, but God's testimony is greater because it is the testimony of God, which he has given about his Son" (v 9).

Thank God that he has given us the testimony of his word in the Bible and his Spirit in our hearts. Say sorry to God for doubting it, and ask him to help you to trust his testimony above all "human testimony".

KEEP IT SIMPLE

"Whoever believes in the Son of God accepts this testimony ... And this is the testimony: God has given us eternal life, and this life is in his Son" (v 10-11).

We might have lots of unanswered questions, but the only thing that ultimately matters is what we think of Jesus: that we believe that eternal life is found in him, the Son of God. Talk to God honestly about what you think of Jesus—tell him now what you believe.

3 REJOICE IN ETERNAL LIFE

"Whoever has the Son has life; whoever does not have the Son of God does not have life" (v 12).

Maybe you sometimes daydream about what life would look like if you gave up on Christianity. But that life would be no life at all. Ask God to give you a real, deep sense of joy in the eternal life he has given you.

4 LISTEN TO YOU

"I write these things to you who believe in the name of the Son of God so that you may know that you have eternal life" (v 13).

Thank God that he wants us to be certain, and he caused the Bible to be written so that we can be. Ask for discipline to keep reading it on your own and meeting with others to hear it taught, however you're feeling. Pray that as you hear God's word, he would grow your assurance that in Christ you have eternal life.

5 SPEAK TO YOU

"This is the confidence we have in approaching God: that if we ask anything according to his will, he hears us" (v 14).

Sometimes praying is the last thing we want to do—but take heart; God hears you. Ask God to keep you making the effort to speak to him in prayer—and pray that as you do so, he would increase your confidence that he hears you.

PRAYING FOR GROWTH WHEN I'M

DISCONTENT

PSALM 73

 CONFESS DISCONTENT

> *"When my heart was grieved and my spirit*
> *embittered, I was senseless and ignorant;*
> *I was a brute beast before you" (v 21-22).*

Tell God what you're discontented about. This psalm invites you to be honest about ways you've "envied" those who have more stuff or fewer problems (v 3), or felt that living God's way is "in vain"—just not worth it (v 13). But it also invites you to realise that thinking this way is ultimately "senseless". Pray that the next four prayer points would convince your heart of this!

 SEE THINGS GOD'S WAY

> *"Then I understood their final destiny ...*
> *How suddenly are they destroyed, com-*
> *pletely swept away by terrors!" (v 17, 19).*

Ask God to help you to see things from an eternal perspective. Pray that next time discontentment bites, you'd remember that whatever material thing you long for now will one day be swept away. Thank God that while others are on "slippery ground" (v 18), by faith you stand secure on the solid rock of his promises.

CONTENT WITH GOD'S PRESENCE

> *"Yet I am always with you; you hold me by my right hand. You guide me with your counsel, and afterwards you will take me into glory" (v 23-24).*

Sometimes we desire good things with good motives; but pray that your greatest joy would always be in being held by God's hand. Give thanks that the majestic Lord of the universe knows you, loves you and cares about you—and that one day, in glory, even the best things of this earth will pale in comparison to seeing him face to face.

 CONTENT WITH MY PORTION

> *"Whom have I in heaven but you? And earth has nothing I desire besides you. My flesh and my heart may fail, but God is the strength of my heart and my portion for ever" (v 25-26).*

Ask God to make these verses real to you—to help you to *really* mean them.

 CONTENTED CONVERSATIONS

> *"I have made the Sovereign LORD my refuge; I will tell of all your deeds" (v 28).*

Often our conversations feed our discontent—so ask God to help you to use your words to point others to God's goodness. Pray that in all your conversations you would grumble less and give thanks more.

PRAYING FOR GROWTH WHEN I'M

OVERWHELMED

NUMBERS 6 v 24-26

PRAYER POINTS:

_____

_____

_____

_____

Father in heaven, when things feel overwhelming, please give me your...

PRESENCE

"The LORD bless you and keep you" (v 24).

Praise God that whatever looms on the horizon, he is the One who keeps you close, lavishes you with love and will never abandon you. Pray that your circumstances would push you into his caring arms—ask to feel a special sense of his presence with you today.

GRACE

"The LORD make his face shine on you and be gracious to you" (v 25).

Thank God for his grace in saving you; he "made his light shine in our hearts to give us the light of the knowledge of God's glory displayed in the face of Christ" (2 Corinthians 4 v 6). Thank God for his grace in giving you good works to do, and gifts to serve him with. Pray that by his grace he would sustain you to walk through whatever lies ahead. Rejoice that when you fall down or fall short, his grace abounds.

3 ATTENTION

"The LORD turn his face towards you..." (v 26).

What is it that God could do to help your situation? Ask God to turn towards you, see your circumstances and act to change them, or to change you.

4 PEACE

"... and give you peace" (v 26).

When we're powerless in the face of problems, or stretched to our limits by our to-do list, we often respond by feeling anxious. Ask God to give you peace—pray that you would be able to trust him with the things that happen, or don't happen. Pray especially that you would be able to sleep well—secure in the knowledge that God has done all that is necessary for our salvation, and that he can accomplish his work despite and even through our weakness.

5 BLESSING

"So they will put my name on the Israelites, and I will bless them" (v 27).

Just as the Israelites belonged to the LORD as his special people, praise God that, in the name of Christ, he has made you his own and showered you with every spiritual blessing—blessings which can never be taken away from you, whatever happens. Pray that your identity as a child of God would hold you steady and give you great joy, even in the midst of stressful times.

PRAYING FOR GROWTH WHEN I'M

SUFFERING

PSALM 25 v 15-22

PRAYER POINTS:

_____

_____

_____

_____

Father, please give me...

 HOPE WHEN I AM DESPERATE

> *"My eyes are ever on the LORD, for only he will release my feet from the snare ... my hope, LORD, is in you" (v 15, 21).*

Thank God that you can fix your eyes on him in your suffering, knowing that he has his eyes fixed on you. Pray that God would use this painful season to set your hope more securely on him, and to cause you to long for the eternity of perfection that he promises.

 COMFORT WHEN I AM LONELY

> *"Turn to me and be gracious to me, for I am lonely and afflicted" (v 16).*

Suffering can be an isolating experience—spiritually, emotionally and socially. If you're feeling alone, ask God to draw near to you, so that you would feel his comfort supernaturally flooding your heart. Thank God for the people you *do* have around you to support you. Pray that you would taste God's grace through God's people, as they love and pray for you.

PEACE WHEN I AM ANXIOUS

"Relieve the troubles of my heart and free me from my anguish" (v 17).

What is it about your situation that is particularly causing you to be anxious? What's the "what-if" that you dread? Bring it before God in prayer now. Ask him to free your mind from the cycles of anxious thoughts and to fill your heart with his peace.

 GRACE WHEN I AM SINFUL

"Look on my affliction and my distress, and take away all my sins" (v 18).

However difficult our circumstances, our greatest need is still for God to take away our sins through Christ. So ask him to do that for you now. Confess the ways in which you have sinned against God and against others in your words, actions and attitudes. Give thanks that Christ bore your sins on the cross and has removed their weight from you for ever.

 REFUGE WHEN I AM IN DANGER

"Guard my life and rescue me; do not let me be put to shame, for I take refuge in you" (v 20).

What in your situation would you like God to rescue you from? Ask him to do it. Then rejoice that whatever happens, in Christ you will never be put to shame—one day you'll stand before your loving Father, completely forgiven and finally free of suffering.

PRAYING FOR GROWTH WHEN I'M

CELEBRATING

1 CHRONICLES 29 v 10-19

PRAYER POINTS:

_____

_____

_____

_____

Father in heaven, as I celebrate, help me to...

WORSHIP YOU

> *"Yours, LORD, is the greatness and the power and the glory and the majesty and the splendour, for everything in heaven and earth is yours" (v 11).*

Take a moment to stand back and worship God for who he is. All the good things we enjoy reveal glimpses of the good God from whom they come—so praise him now.

GIVE YOU THE CREDIT

> *"Wealth and honour come from you ... In your hands are strength and power to exalt and give strength to all" (v 12).*

Thank God for his generosity. Confess any self-glorying in your achievements that you may be indulging in; ask God to give you a greater awareness that everything—your gifts and successes—comes from his hands. Echo David: "Now, our God, we give you thanks, and praise your glorious name" (v 13).

BE GENEROUS

"But who am I ... that we should be able to give as generously as this? Everything comes from you, and we have given you only what comes from your hand" (v 14).

This good thing likely gives you new opportunities to be generous—perhaps with your time, money, home, family or love. What might that look like for you? Ask God to prompt you to take these opportunities. Pray that, like David, you would view the opportunity to be generous as a God-given privilege.

 STOP CHASING SHADOWS

"Our days on earth are like a shadow" (v 15).

Ask God to maintain your eternal perspective. Ask him to humble you as you reflect on the shortness and smallness of this life, and to cause you to rejoice that even the best things here are mere shadows compared to the dazzling reality of what is yet to come.

 DEVOTE MY HEART TO YOU

"Keep these desires and thoughts in the hearts of your people for ever, and keep their hearts loyal to you" (v 18).

Whatever your hopes and ambitions for the months and years ahead, pray that your greatest desire would be to honour Christ. In what way might your loyalty to him be tested? Ask God to give you "the whole-hearted devotion to keep [his] commands" (v 19).

PRAYING FOR GROWTH WHEN I'M
GETTING OLDER

PHILIPPIANS 3 v 12-14

PRAYER POINTS:

Here's one for birthdays, New Years, anniversaries, and any time you're feeling your age!

 HELD

> *"I press on to take hold of that for which Christ Jesus took hold of me" (v 12).*

Look back and thank Jesus for how he first took hold of you when you became a Christian. Praise him for the way he's kept hold of you through the twists and turns of life in the years and months since. Give thanks for specific seasons or moments when you have particularly felt his loving grip on you.

 HUMBLE

> *"I do not consider myself yet to have taken hold of it" (v 13).*

This side of eternity, no one has "arrived" as a Christian. Repent of any ways in which you've grown complacent in your faith. Confess times when you've felt proud of what you've achieved, or settled for compromise instead of striving to grow. Ask God to show you how he wants to make you more like Christ.

NO REGRETS

> *"… forgetting what is behind and straining towards what is ahead…" (v 13).*

As you look back, what is it that you regret? Maybe it's something you did, or something you didn't do. Thank God that he has dealt with your past sin—ask him to help you to "forget" it, now he's forgiven it. Thank him that your best days are ahead of you in eternity, not behind you in this life.

 NO DISTRACTIONS

> *"But one thing I do … I press on towards the goal" (v 13-14).*

Pray that faithfully following Jesus every day of your life would be the "one thing" you do. What threatens to distract you from that great aim? What draws your eyes away from the goal? Ask God to give you a wholehearted determination to keep serving Christ.

 WIN THE PRIZE

> *"… to win the prize for which God has called me heavenwards in Christ Jesus" (v 14).*

Thank God that you're heading for a prize so much better than checking off the next big life milestone, or a gold-plated pension, or the holiday of a lifetime— you're heading to meet Jesus in heaven! Spend some time rejoicing in that truth now. Pray that, by God's grace, you would walk by faith until you hold that prize.

OTHER BOOKS IN THIS SERIES

"A THOUGHT-PROVOKING, VISION-
EXPANDING, PRAYER-STIMULATING
TOOL. SIMPLE, BUT BRILLIANT."

SINCLAIR FERGUSON

thegoodbook
COMPANY

BIBLICAL | RELEVANT | ACCESSIBLE

At The Good Book Company, we are dedicated to helping Christians and local churches grow. We believe that God's growth process always starts with hearing clearly what he has said to us through his timeless word—the Bible.

Ever since we opened our doors in 1991, we have been striving to produce resources that honour God in the way the Bible is used. We have grown to become an international provider of user-friendly resources to the Christian community, with believers of all backgrounds and denominations using our Bible studies, books, evangelistic resources, DVD-based courses and training events.

We want to equip ordinary Christians to live for Christ day by day, and churches to grow in their knowledge of God, their love for one another, and the effectiveness of their outreach.

Call us for a discussion of your needs or visit one of our local websites for more information on the resources and services we provide.

Your friends at The Good Book Company

UK & EUROPE
NORTH AMERICA
AUSTRALIA
NEW ZEALAND

thegoodbook.co.uk
thegoodbook.com
thegoodbook.com.au
thegoodbook.co.nz

0333 123 0880
866 244 2165
(02) 9564 3555

WWW.CHRISTIANITYEXPLORED.ORG
Our partner site is a great place for those exploring the Christian faith, with a clear explanation of the good news, powerful testimonies and answers to difficult questions.